# The River Nene

## Peterborough to Northampton
including the Grand Union Canal
(Northampton Arm to Gayton Junction)

**Imray Laurie Norie & Wilson Ltd**
St Ives Huntingdon England

Published by
**Imray, Laurie, Norie & Wilson Ltd**
Wych House, St Ives, Huntingdon,
Cambridgeshire PE17 4BT, England
☎ (01480) 462114
*Fax* (01480) 496109
1999

British Library Cataloguing in Publication
Data.
A catalogue record for this book is available
from the British Library.

ISBN 0 85288 431 1

CAUTION
Every effort has been taken to ensure the
accuracy of this book. It contains selected
information and thus is not definitive and
does not include all known information on
the subject in hand; this is particularly
relevant to the plans which should not be
used for navigation. The author and
publisher believe that its selection is a useful
aid to prudent navigation but the safety of a
vessel depends ultimately on the judgement
of the navigator who should assess all
information, published or unpublished,
available to him.

These notes are reproduced with permission
from *Navigations in the Anglian Region*,
published by the Environment Agency.

This work has been corrected to November
1999

Printed in Great Britain by
Imray Laurie Norie & Wilson Ltd

# KEY  TO SYMBOLS USED ON THE MAPS

## Scale approximately 3″ to 1 mile

| | |
|---|---|
| | Moorings |
| | Slipway |
| | Direction of stream |
| | Post Office |
| | Telephone |
| | Lock |
| | Weir |
| | Information |
| | Pump out |
| | Toilet |
| | Public House |
| | Fuel |
| | Water |
| | Church |
| | Station |
| | Showers |
| | Power Cable |
| | Footpath |

# BOAT LICENSING AND REGISTRATION

## River Nene

Details of regional requirements for the registration and licensing of craft to use the waterways described in this booklet are available from:

Environment Agency
Anglian Region
Kingfisher House
Goldhay Way
Orton Goldhay
Peterborough PE2 5ZR
☎ (01733) 371811

Boat owners navigating Recreational Waterways within the Environment Agency's Anglian Region should acquaint themselves with the following legislation, copies of which can be obtained from the Environment Agency at the above address.

*The Recreational Waterways (Registration) Byelaws 1979*

*The Recreational Waterways (General) Byelaws 1980*

## Grand Union Canal

British Waterways
Marsworth Junction
Watery Lane
Marsworth
Tring HP23 4LZ
☎ (01442) 825938

# RIVER NENE NAVIGATION

The River Nene is a particularly important navigation as it links the Grand Union Canal to the Middle Level and the sea. Although the navigation was originally commercial it is now almost entirely used for recreation.

Flowing through Northamptonshire, Cambridgeshire, Lincolnshire and bordering Norfolk, the Nene gives contrasting views of eastern England. In Northamptonshire the river flows through farmland and the industry of Northampton, Wellingborough and Irthlingborough interspersed with the numerous stone villages with their churches for which this 'county of squires and spires' is famous.

Peterborough dominates the route through Cambridgeshire with the cathedral visible on the horizon across the fenland landscape. The Nene was tidal to Peterborough until the construction of the tidal lock and sluice at the Dog-in-a-Doublet in 1937.

The tidal Nene flows through parts of Lincolnshire to the busy port of Wisbech with its Dutch style waterfront architecture and the new port at Sutton Bridge before entering the Wash between two towers known as 'the lighthouses'.

Rising at sources near Badby, Naseby and Yelvertoft, the Nene becomes navigable at Northampton where these tributaries combine. Navigation begins at the junction with the Northampton Arm of the Grand Union Canal near Cotten End Lock and extends 91 miles (147km) to the sea.

The Agency's Recreational Waterway stretches from Northampton to Bevis Hall, just upstream of Wisbech. River users must conform to the Recreational Byelaws throughout this length.

Boat traffic is increasing on this attractive waterway but it is still quiet compared with other navigations such as the canals and Great Ouse.

A speed limit of 7mph (11kmph) applies throughout the navigation except for one mile downstream of Peterborough. This derestricted stretch is clearly signposted.

There are 66 fixed bridges and 37 locks between Peterborough and Northampton. Each lock is 83ft 6ins (25·5m) long and 15ft wide (4·6m). To make allowances for adverse conditions, the maximum, dimensions for craft should be regarded as:

*Length* 78ft (23m)
*Beam* 13ft (3·9m)
*Draught* 4ft (1·2m)
*Headroom* 7ft (2·1m)

All craft approaching these maximum dimensions would have difficulties.

Water levels cannot be guaranteed. Care should be taken when:

1. Approaching any of the river controls, weirs, sluices, locks etc, should there be any significant flow on the river.
2. Stopping overnight, or leaving a boat for a considerable length of time – i.e. over winter (where boats are permitted to remain in the water) – or in a flood situation, do not moor in shallow water or with a tight rope or chain as water levels may fluctuate. If the level drops and a craft is moored aground or in shallow water, it may be careened or damaged. If the level rises and mooring ropes or chains are tight, the boat may take on water, be pulled under or even broken

## RIVER NENE

### Northampton to Peterborough

*Distance* 57.3 miles (92.2km)
*Length* 78' (23.7m)
*Beam* 13' (3.9m)
*Draught* 4' (1.2m
*Headroom* 7' (2.1m)
*Locks* 37

## GRAND UNION CANAL
### Northampton Arm
Gayton to Northampton

*Distance* 4.8 miles (7.7km)
*Length* 72' (21.9m)
*Beam* 7' (2.1m)
*Draught* 2' 6'' (0.8m)
*Headroom* 7' (2.1m)
*Locks* 17

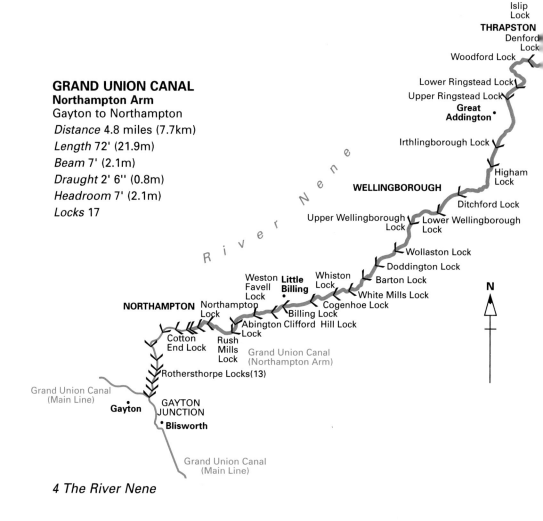

Islip Lock
**THRAPSTON**
Denford Lock
Woodford Lock
Lower Ringstead Lock
Upper Ringstead Lock
**Great Addington**
Irthlingborough Lock
Higham Lock
**WELLINGBOROUGH**
Ditchford Lock
Upper Wellingborough Lock
Lower Wellingborough Lock
Wollaston Lock
Doddington Lock
Barton Lock
Whiston Lock
White Mills Lock
Weston Favell Lock
**Little Billing**
Cogenhoe Lock
**NORTHAMPTON**
Northampton Lock
Billing Lock
Clifford Hill Lock
Abington Lock
Cotton End Lock
Rush Mills Lock
Grand Union Canal (Northampton Arm)
Rothersthorpe Locks (13)
Grand Union Canal (Main Line)
**Gayton**
GAYTON JUNCTION
**Blisworth**
Grand Union Canal (Main Line)

N

*4 The River Nene*

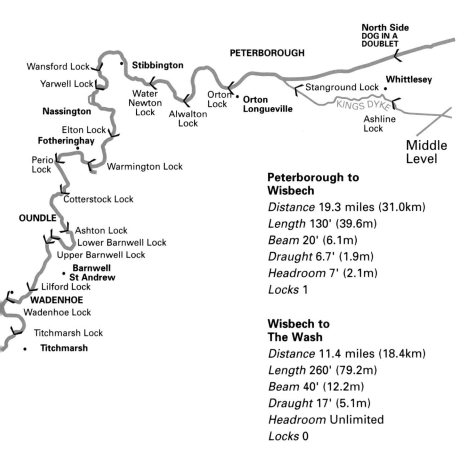

**PETERBOROUGH**

North Side
DOG IN A
DOUBLET

Wansford Lock
Yarwell Lock
**Stibbington**
Water Newton Lock
Alwalton Lock
Orton Lock
**Orton Longueville**
Stanground Lock
**Whittlesey**
KINGS DYKE
Ashline Lock

Middle Level

**Nassington**
Elton Lock
**Fotheringhay**
Perio Lock
Warmington Lock
Cotterstock Lock
**OUNDLE**
Ashton Lock
Lower Barnwell Lock
Upper Barnwell Lock
**Barnwell St Andrew**
Lilford Lock
**WADENHOE**
Wadenhoe Lock
Titchmarsh Lock
**Titchmarsh**

## Peterborough to Wisbech

*Distance* 19.3 miles (31.0km)
*Length* 130' (39.6m)
*Beam* 20' (6.1m)
*Draught* 6.7' (1.9m)
*Headroom* 7' (2.1m)
*Locks* 1

## Wisbech to The Wash

*Distance* 11.4 miles (18.4km)
*Length* 260' (79.2m)
*Beam* 40' (12.2m)
*Draught* 17' (5.1m)
*Headroom* Unlimited
*Locks* 0

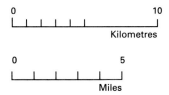

0                    10
Kilometres

0          5
Miles

free. The Environment Agency (Anglian Region) is not liable for any damage caused to craft moored on the river, as a result of fluctuating water levels.

## Mooring

Boats must not be moored within 36m of any locks, sluices, weirs or water intakes except when navigating through a lock. In some cases such as the Dog-in-a-Doublet, Bedford Road Sluice (Northampton) and Weston Favel (Northampton) mooring is prohibited for 100m on both sides of the structure.

The Nene is a Recreational Waterway between Cotton End Lock, Northampton and Bevis Hall, Wisbech and Environment Agency Recreational Bye-laws apply to all of this length of river.

## River Nene locks

The majority of River Nene locks have steel pointing doors at the upstream end and vertical gates at the lower end.

Locks should be left with the pointing doors closed and the vertical lift gate raised and locked.

The vertical gates are normally locked. Keys are therefore required to operate the locks on the River Nene. These can be obtained from the Environment Agency, Anglian Region, Kingfisher House, Goldhay Way, Orton Goldhay, Peterborough, Cambs PE2 5ZR. Two weeks should be allowed to process applications. A windlass to fit a 1¼ inch square is required to operate the paddles.

## Using the locks

The vertical steel gates should be operated with care. Children should not be allowed to operate them. At the first operation, *always* take the weight of the gate carefully, using both hands. This will avoid the risk of injury in the event of unauthorised interference with the counter-balance weights. Boat owners are advised to use side fenders when inside the lock pen, to avoid damage on the mooring chain bolts.

**Procedure when entering the lock from the higher level**
- Lower the vertical gate
- Open paddles in the pointing doors
- Open the pointing doors when water levels are equal, and enter the lock
- Lower the paddles and close the pointing doors

- Raise the vertical door a few inches only. This is stiff at first, to prevent rapid opening of the door and possible boat damage. The vertical gate should be *fully raised* once the water level in the lock pen has fallen

**Procedure when entering the lock from a lower level**
- After entering the lock, lower the vertical gate
- Open paddles in the pointing doors
- When levels permit, open the pointing doors
- After leaving the lock, lower the paddles and close the pointing door
- Finally, *raise the vertical gate fully.*

**Caution** If the pointing doors are found chained back (open) and the vertical gate partially lifted, ie the lock is 'reversed', no attempt to navigate should be made. Warning signs are sited upstream and downstream of locks to indicate when a lock is reversed.

Should there have been heavy rain in the area it is probable there will be a rapid change in water condition eg rise in level, increase in current, change in colour. With any such change in conditions the Agency will almost certainly be operating sluices to regulate water levels and extreme care should be taken when approaching locks or other structures.

## Useful telephone numbers

**Dog-in-a-Doublet Locks**
☎ (01733) 202219
**British Waterways**, Blisworth,
Northampton ☎ (01604) 858233
**Stanground Lock-keeper**, Peterborough
☎ (01733) 566413
**Middle Level Commissioners**, March
☎ (01354) 653232
**Port of Wisbech**, Wisbech
☎ (01954) 582125
**Environment Agency Office, Kettering**,
☎ (01536) 517721
**Environment Agency Office, Spalding**,
☎ (01775) 762123
**East Northamptonshire Council,
Tourist Information**, Oundle
☎ (01832) 274333

## Slipways

**Billing Aquadrome** ☎ (01604) 408181
**Frontiers Activity Centre**
☎ (01933) 651718
**Ken Yates Marine Sales**, Billing
Aquadrome ☎ (01604) 408312
**Middle Nene Cruising Club** (available for
club members)
**Northampton Boat Club** (available for
club members)
**EA Public Slipway**, Turnells Mill Lane,
Wellingborough ☎ (01536) 517721
**Oundle Marina** ☎ (01832) 272762
**Peterborough Boating Centre**, 73 North
Street, Stanground, Peterborough
☎ (01733) 566688
**Peterborough City Council** (Public
Slipway), Potters Way, Fengate,
Peterborough ☎ (01733) 563141 (office
hours)
**Peterborough Cruising Club**
☎ (01733) 232739
**Peterborough Yacht Club** (available for
club members)
**The Queens Head, Nassington**,
☎ (01780) 782289
**Stibbington Boatyard** ☎ (01780) 783144
**Thrapston Mill Marina**,
☎ (01832) 732850
**Yarwell Mill**, ☎ (01780) 782247

## Short-term points and lock key agencies, River Nene and Grand Union Canal

**Blisworth Tunnel Boats**, Northampton
☎ (01604) 858868
**Grand Junction Boat Co,** Northampton,
☎ (01604) 858043
**Alvechurch Boats**, Gayton Marina,
Northampton ☎ (01604) 858685
**Ken Yates Marine Sales**, Billing
Aquadrome, Northampton
☎ (01604) 408312
**Peterborough Boating Centre**, 73 North
Street, Stanground, Peterborough
☎ (01733) 566688
**Mike Wright**, Dog-in-a-Doublet Sluice
Bungalow, Peterborough ☎ (01733)
202219
**Anchor Cottage Crafts** (Licences), Long
Buckby,
☎ (01327) 842140

## Other marine services

**Princess Yachts and Marine Secol**,
☎ (01604) 890559
**Cogenhoe Mill**, Northampton
☎ (01604) 890579
**Thrapston Mill Marina**, Thrapston
☎ (01832) 732850
**Oundle Marina**, Oundle
☎ (01832) 272762
**Yarwell Mill**, Stamford
☎ (01780) 782247
**Stibbington Boatyard**, Stamford
☎ (01780) 783144

**River Nene. Distances in Miles**
*Northampton, junction with Northampton
Branch of the Grand Union Canal to:*

| | |
|---|---|
| Northampton, South Bridge | 0.1 |
| Northampton Lock No 1 | 0.4 |
| Rush Mills Lock No 2 | 1.6 |
| Abington Lock No 3 | 2.0 |
| Weston Favell Lock No 4 | 2.9 |
| Clifford Hill Lock No 5 | 3.7 |
| Billing Lock No 6 | 4.3 |
| Cogenhoe Lock No 7 | 5.4 |
| Whiston Lock No 8 | 6.5 |
| White Mills Lock No 9 | 7.2 |
| Barton Lock No 10 | 8.1 |
| Doddington Lock No 11 | 8.8 |
| Wollaston Lock No 12 | 9.9 |
| Upper Wellingborough Lock No 13 | 11.2 |
| A45 Bridge | 11.3 |
| Lower Wellingborough Lock No 14 | 12.1 |
| Ditchford Lock No 15 | 13.9 |
| Higham Lock No 16 | 15.9 |
| Irthlingborough Bridge | 16.3 |
| Irthlingborough Lock No 17 | 16.8 |
| Upper Ringstead Lock No 18 | 19.1 |
| Lower Ringstead Lock No 19 | 19.7 |
| Woodford Lock No 20 | 21.9 |
| Denford Lock No 21 | 22.8 |
| A14 Bridge | 23.4 |
| Islip Lock No 22 | 24.2 |
| Titchmarsh Lock No 23 | 26.3 |
| Wadenhoe Lock No 24 | 28.7 |
| Lilford Lock No 25 | 29.7 |
| Upper Barnwell Lock No 26 | 31.9 |
| Lower Barnwell Lock No 27 | 32.3 |
| Ashton Lock No 28 | 34.1 |
| Oundle Bridge | 35.0 |
| Cotterstock Lock No 29 | 36.2 |
| Perio Lock No 30 | 38.0 |
| Warmington Lock No 31 | 40.4 |
| Elton Lock No 32 | 42.0 |
| Yarwell Lock No 33 | 45.0 |
| Wansford Lock No 34 | 46.2 |
| A1 Bridge | 46.9 |
| Waternewton Lock No 35 | 49.9 |
| Alwalton Lock No 36 | 51.7 |
| Orton Lock No 37 | 55.4 |
| Peterborough Bridge | 57.3 |
| Peterborough, junction with Branch to Stanground and Middle Level Navigations | 57.9 |
| Dog-in-a-Doublet (inn) Lock No 38 (power-operated, with emergency hand operation) | 62.5 |
| Popley's Gull | 64.2 |
| Guyhirn | 70.6 |
| Bevis Hall | 74.0 |
| Wisbech Town | 76.6 |
| Junction with North Level Main Drain | 81.9 |
| Junction with South Holland Main Drain (sluice entrance is only opened at flood times) | 83.2 |
| Sutton Bridge | 83.9 |
| Guy's Head 'Lighthouses' | 86.9 |
| The Wash at Crabs Hole, mouth of river | 88.0 |

**Grand Union Canal. Distances in Miles**
*Gayton Junction,
junction with the Main Line to:*

| | |
|---|---|
| Gayton Marina | 0.1 |
| Milton Road Bridge No 3 | 0.5 |
| Rothersthorpe Top Lock No 1 | 0.7 |
| Rothersthorpe Bottom Lock No 13 | 1.7 |
| Wootton Lock No 14 | 2.1 |
| Hardingstone Lock No 15 | 3.0 |
| Duston Mill Bridge No 13 and Hunsbury Hill Industrial Museum | 3.3 |
| Northampton Lock No 16 | 4.1 |
| Cotton End Lock No 17, junction with River Nene | 4.8 |

# For passage to and from the tidal River Nene

The river is tidal for 25 miles downstream of the Dog-in-a-Doublet Lock which is five miles below Peterborough. Registered craft may pass through this lock every day from 0730 hours until official sunset time. Boat owners are advised to telephone the lock-keeper at Peterborough ☎ (01733) 202219, in advance of their arrival to make arrangements for passage. Passage before 0730 and after sunset by prior arrangement and a £6 charge.

For information in respect of the passage of craft or moorings in the port of Wisbech and down to the sea apply to:

The Port Manager
Port Office
Wisbech ☎(01945) 582125

Craft should proceed through Wisbech with care. The banks are lined with steel and concrete piling, there is stone in the bed, and there is a strong run on the flood and ebb tide, particularly at the lower stages.

## River Nene downstream of Peterborough Embankment

Below the junction with Stanground Backwater there is a single span road bridge and then a double span bridge Fitzwilliam Bridge which marks the beginning of the derestricted mile where no speed limit applies. The length is clearly signed at both ends but extreme caution is required especially when water skiing is in progress. Skiing and speeding outside this derestricted zone will lead to prosecution.

At the end of the mile there are two bends before a straight 2 mile channel leads to the tidal Dog-in-a-Doublet lock.

### Dog-in-a-Doublet Locks

These are manned most daylight hours. No mooring is permitted within 100 metres of the lock except in passage. Water point and toilet facilities are available with a lock key. A pay phone is available in the lock control building

The nearby Dog-in-a-Doublet public house has a restaurant and there are good facilities in Whittlesey, one mile to the south.

### The Tidal River

Only Guyhirn (8 miles), Wisbech (15 miles) and Sutton Bridge (23 miles) lie on the river downstream of the Dog-in-a-Doublet. Add 2 hours to times for tides listed for West Lighthouse to the Dog-in-a-Doublet.

Headroom clearance at Guyhirn Road Bridge varies with state of tide.

There is an outfall from Whittlesey Washes (Moreton's Leam) above Guyhirn on the right bank and the North Level Drain and South Holland Drains discharge on the left bank between Wisbech and Sutton Bridge.

There is a strong run on the flood and ebb tides in Wisbech and boats should avoid these periods.

North Side

B1040

Dog-in-a-Doublet PH

Whittlesey
EC Thurs
Shops

**DOG-IN-A-DOUBLET SEA LOCK**
Lock-keeper
☎ 01733 202219

Guyhirn (8 miles)
Wisbech (15 miles)

Nene Way

River Nene

Gull Farm

Plum Tree Farm

Roslyn Farm

N

0 ⟶ 1

Mile (Approx)

Northey Rd

Nene Way

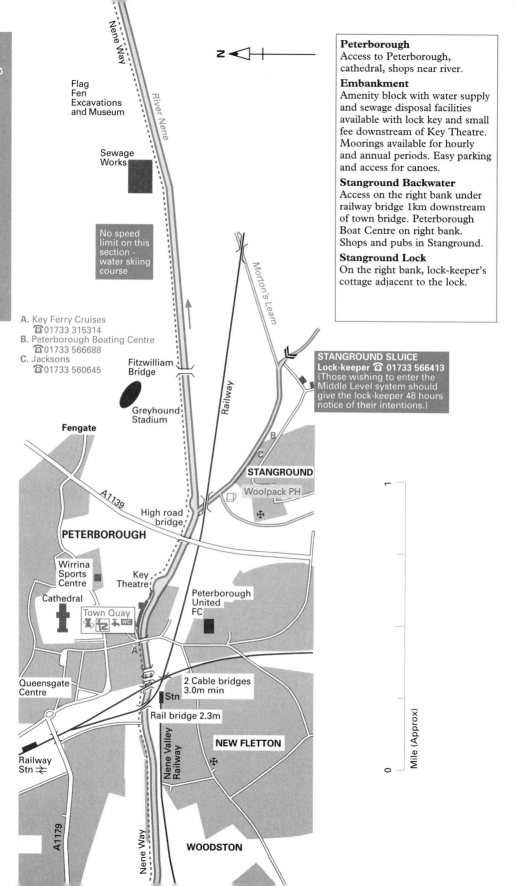

N

**Nene Way**

**Flag Fen Excavations and Museum**

**River Nene**

**Sewage Works**

No speed limit on this section - water skiing course

A. Key Ferry Cruises ☎ 01733 315314
B. Peterborough Boating Centre ☎ 01733 566688
C. Jacksons ☎ 01733 560645

**Fitzwilliam Bridge**

**Greyhound Stadium**

**Fengate**

A1139

**High road bridge**

**PETERBOROUGH**

Wirrina Sports Centre

Key Theatre

Cathedral

Town Quay

Peterborough United FC

Queensgate Centre

A

2 Cable bridges 3.0m min

Stn

Rail bridge 2.3m

**NEW FLETTON**

Railway Stn

Nene Valley Railway

A1179

Nene Way

**WOODSTON**

**Morton's Leam**

**Railway**

B

C

**STANGROUND**

Woolpack PH

**STANGROUND SLUICE**
Lock-keeper ☎ **01733 566413**
(Those wishing to enter the Middle Level system should give the lock-keeper 48 hours notice of their intentions.)

1

Mile (Approx)

0

**Peterborough**
Access to Peterborough, cathedral, shops near river.

**Embankment**
Amenity block with water supply and sewage disposal facilities available with lock key and small fee downstream of Key Theatre. Moorings available for hourly and annual periods. Easy parking and access for canoes.

**Stanground Backwater**
Access on the right bank under railway bridge 1km downstream of town bridge. Peterborough Boat Centre on right bank. Shops and pubs in Stanground.

**Stanground Lock**
On the right bank, lock-keeper's cottage adjacent to the lock.

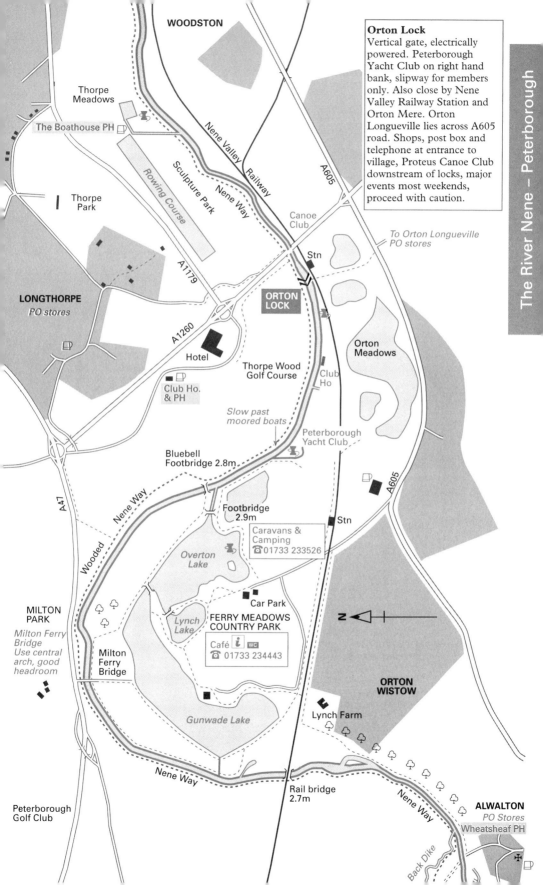

WOODSTON

Thorpe Meadows

The Boathouse PH

Nene Valley Railway

A605

Rowing Course

Sculpture Park

Nene Way

Thorpe Park

**Orton Lock**
Vertical gate, electrically powered. Peterborough Yacht Club on right hand bank, slipway for members only. Also close by Nene Valley Railway Station and Orton Mere. Orton Longueville lies across A605 road. Shops, post box and telephone at entrance to village, Proteus Canoe Club downstream of locks, major events most weekends, proceed with caution.

Canoe Club

To Orton Longueville PO stores

Stn

**LONGTHORPE**
*PO stores*

A1179

A1260

Hotel

ORTON LOCK

Orton Meadows

Club Ho. & PH

Thorpe Wood Golf Course

Club Ho

*Slow past moored boats*

Peterborough Yacht Club

Bluebell Footbridge 2.8m

A605

A47

Nene Way

Wooded

Footbridge 2.9m

Stn

Caravans & Camping
☎ 01733 233526

*Overton Lake*

Car Park

**MILTON PARK**

*Milton Ferry Bridge*
*Use central arch, good headroom*

*Lynch Lake*

Milton Ferry Bridge

**FERRY MEADOWS COUNTRY PARK**

Café ℹ wc
☎ 01733 234443

N

**ORTON WISTOW**

*Gunwade Lake*

Lynch Farm

Nene Way

Peterborough Golf Club

Rail bridge 2.7m

Nene Way

**ALWALTON**
*PO Stores*
Wheatsheaf PH

*Back Dike*

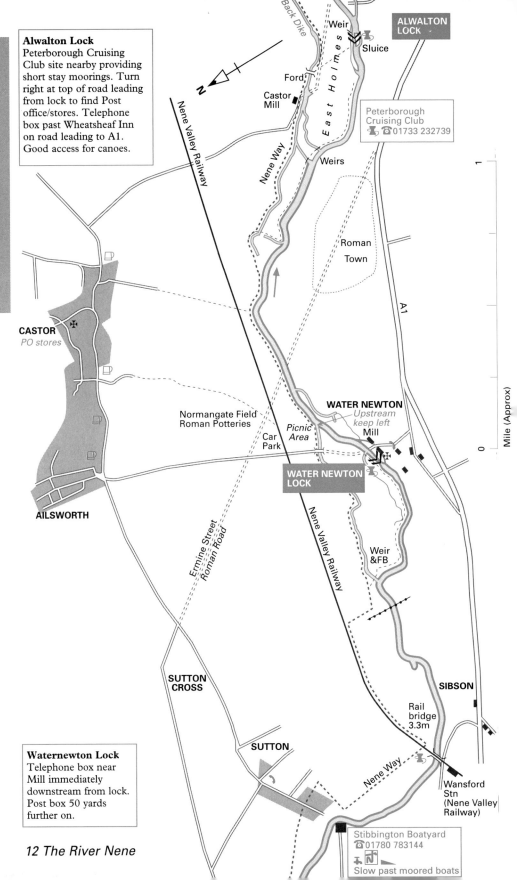

**Alwalton Lock**
Peterborough Cruising
Club site nearby providing
short stay moorings. Turn
right at top of road leading
from lock to find Post
office/stores. Telephone
box past Wheatsheaf Inn
on road leading to A1.
Good access for canoes.

Back Dike

Weir

**ALWALTON LOCK**

Sluice

Ford

Castor
Mill

*E a s t   H o l m e s*

Peterborough
Cruising Club
☎ 01733 232739

Nene Valley Railway

Nene Way

Weirs

Roman
Town

A1

CASTOR
*PO stores*

Normangate Field
Roman Potteries

Car
Park

*Picnic
Area*

**WATER NEWTON**
*Upstream
keep left*
Mill

AILSWORTH

Ermine Street
Roman Road

**WATER NEWTON
LOCK**

Nene Valley Railway

Weir
&FB

Mile (Approx)

1

0

SUTTON
CROSS

SIBSON

Rail
bridge
3.3m

SUTTON

Nene Way

Wansford
Stn
(Nene Valley
Railway)

**Waternewton Lock**
Telephone box near
Mill immediately
downstream from lock.
Post box 50 yards
further on.

Stibbington Boatyard
☎ 01780 783144

Slow past moored boats

*12 The River Nene*

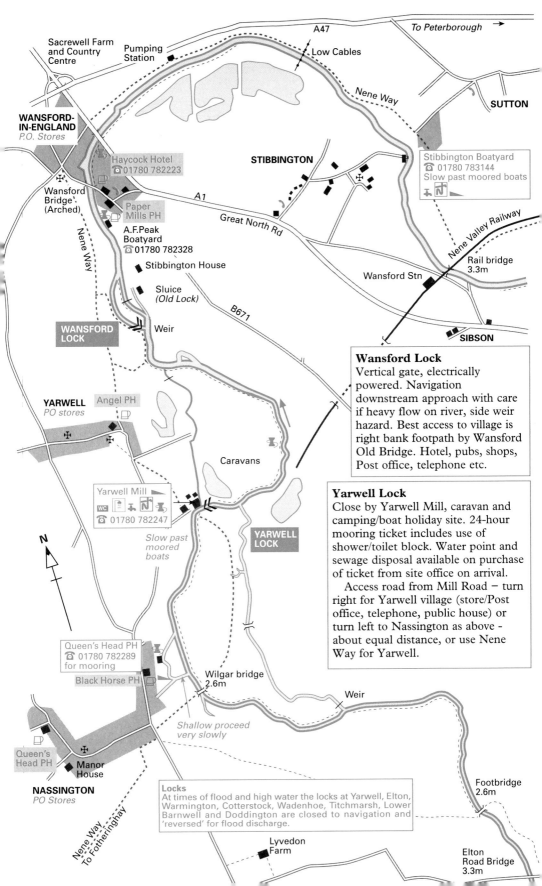

To Peterborough →

A47

Low Cables

Nene Way

SUTTON

Sacrewell Farm and Country Centre

Pumping Station

STIBBINGTON

Stibbington Boatyard
☎ 01780 783144
Slow past moored boats

WANSFORD-IN-ENGLAND
*P.O. Stores*

Haycock Hotel
☎ 01780 782223

Nene Valley Railway

A1

Great North Rd

Wansford Bridge (Arched)

Paper Mills PH

A.F.Peak Boatyard
☎ 01780 782328

Rail bridge 3.3m

Wansford Stn

Stibbington House

Nene Way

Sluice (Old Lock)

B671

SIBSON

WANSFORD LOCK

Weir

**Wansford Lock**
Vertical gate, electrically powered. Navigation downstream approach with care if heavy flow on river, side weir hazard. Best access to village is right bank footpath by Wansford Old Bridge. Hotel, pubs, shops, Post office, telephone etc.

YARWELL
*PO stores*

Angel PH

Caravans

**Yarwell Lock**
Close by Yarwell Mill, caravan and camping/boat holiday site. 24-hour mooring ticket includes use of shower/toilet block. Water point and sewage disposal available on purchase of ticket from site office on arrival.

Access road from Mill Road – turn right for Yarwell village (store/Post office, telephone, public house) or turn left to Nassington as above - about equal distance, or use Nene Way for Yarwell.

Yarwell Mill
☎ 01780 782247

Slow past moored boats

YARWELL LOCK

N

Queen's Head PH
☎ 01780 782289
for mooring

Black Horse PH

Wilgar bridge 2.6m

Weir

Shallow proceed very slowly

Queen's Head PH

Manor House

NASSINGTON
*PO stores*

Footbridge 2.6m

**Locks**
At times of flood and high water the locks at Yarwell, Elton, Warmington, Cotterstock, Wadenhoe, Titchmarsh, Lower Barnwell and Doddington are closed to navigation and 'reversed' for flood discharge.

Nene Way To Fotheringhay

Lyvedon Farm

Elton Road Bridge 3.3m

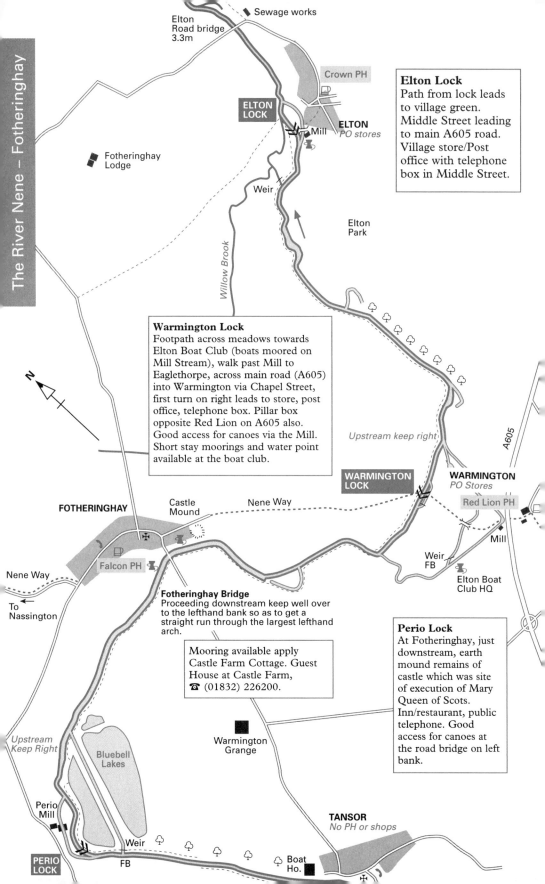

Sewage works

Elton
Road bridge
3.3m

Crown PH

**ELTON
LOCK**

Fotheringhay
Lodge

Mill

**ELTON**
*PO stores*

Weir

Elton
Park

Willow Brook

**Elton Lock**
Path from lock leads
to village green.
Middle Street leading
to main A605 road.
Village store/Post
office with telephone
box in Middle Street.

**Warmington Lock**
Footpath across meadows towards
Elton Boat Club (boats moored on
Mill Stream), walk past Mill to
Eaglethorpe, across main road (A605)
into Warmington via Chapel Street,
first turn on right leads to store, post
office, telephone box. Pillar box
opposite Red Lion on A605 also.
Good access for canoes via the Mill.
Short stay moorings and water point
available at the boat club.

N

*Upstream keep right*

A605

**WARMINGTON
LOCK**

**WARMINGTON**
*PO Stores*

Red Lion PH

**FOTHERINGHAY**

Castle
Mound

Nene Way

Mill

Nene Way

Falcon PH

Weir
FB

To
Nassington

Elton Boat
Club HQ

**Fotheringhay Bridge**
Proceeding downstream keep well over
to the lefthand bank so as to get a
straight run through the largest lefthand
arch.

Mooring available apply
Castle Farm Cottage. Guest
House at Castle Farm,
☎ (01832) 226200.

**Perio Lock**
At Fotheringhay, just
downstream, earth
mound remains of
castle which was site
of execution of Mary
Queen of Scots.
Inn/restaurant, public
telephone. Good
access for canoes at
the road bridge on left
bank.

*Upstream
Keep Right*

Bluebell
Lakes

Warmington
Grange

Perio
Mill

Weir

**TANSOR**
*No PH or shops*

**PERIO
LOCK**

FB

Boat
Ho.

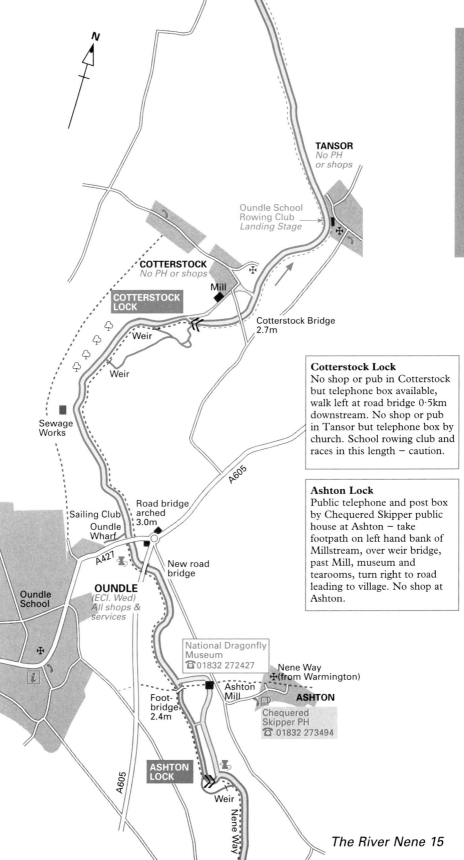

Mile (Approx)

0  1

N

**TANSOR**
*No PH or shops*

Oundle School
Rowing Club
*Landing Stage*

**COTTERSTOCK**
*No PH or shops*

Mill

**COTTERSTOCK LOCK**

Weir

Weir

Cotterstock Bridge
2.7m

Sewage Works

A605

**Cotterstock Lock**
No shop or pub in Cotterstock
but telephone box available,
walk left at road bridge 0·5km
downstream. No shop or pub
in Tansor but telephone box by
church. School rowing club and
races in this length – caution.

**Ashton Lock**
Public telephone and post box
by Chequered Skipper public
house at Ashton – take
footpath on left hand bank of
Millstream, over weir bridge,
past Mill, museum and
tearooms, turn right to road
leading to village. No shop at
Ashton.

Sailing Club
Oundle Wharf

Road bridge arched
3.0m

A427

New road bridge

Oundle School

**OUNDLE**
*(Ecl. Wed)
All shops &
services*

National Dragonfly
Museum
☎ 01832 272427

Nene Way
(from Warmington)

Foot-bridge
2.4m

Ashton Mill

**ASHTON**

Chequered
Skipper PH
☎ 01832 273494

A605

**ASHTON LOCK**

Weir

Nene Way

*The River Nene 15*

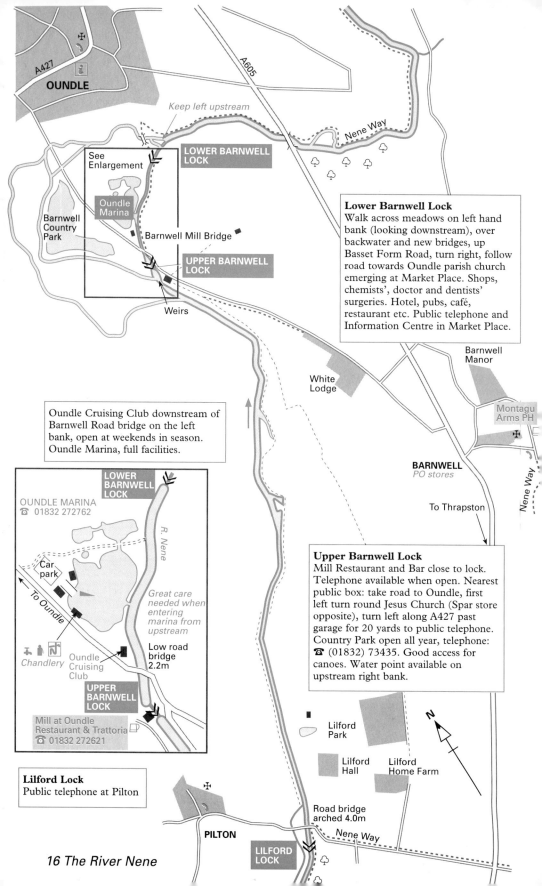

OUNDLE

A427

A605

Keep left upstream

Nene Way

LOWER BARNWELL LOCK

See Enlargement

Oundle Marina

Barnwell Country Park

Barnwell Mill Bridge

UPPER BARNWELL LOCK

Weirs

**Lower Barnwell Lock**
Walk across meadows on left hand bank (looking downstream), over backwater and new bridges, up Basset Form Road, turn right, follow road towards Oundle parish church emerging at Market Place. Shops, chemists', doctor and dentists' surgeries. Hotel, pubs, café, restaurant etc. Public telephone and Information Centre in Market Place.

Barnwell Manor

White Lodge

Montagu Arms PH

BARNWELL
PO stores

To Thrapston

Oundle Cruising Club downstream of Barnwell Road bridge on the left bank, open at weekends in season. Oundle Marina, full facilities.

LOWER BARNWELL LOCK

OUNDLE MARINA
☎ 01832 272762

R. Nene

Car park

To Oundle

Great care needed when entering marina from upstream

Chandlery

Oundle Cruising Club

Low road bridge 2.2m

UPPER BARNWELL LOCK

Mill at Oundle Restaurant & Trattoria
☎ 01832 272621

**Upper Barnwell Lock**
Mill Restaurant and Bar close to lock. Telephone available when open. Nearest public box: take road to Oundle, first left turn round Jesus Church (Spar store opposite), turn left along A427 past garage for 20 yards to public telephone. Country Park open all year, telephone: ☎ (01832) 73435. Good access for canoes. Water point available on upstream right bank.

Lilford Park

Lilford Hall

Lilford Home Farm

N

**Lilford Lock**
Public telephone at Pilton

PILTON

Road bridge arched 4.0m

Nene Way

LILFORD LOCK

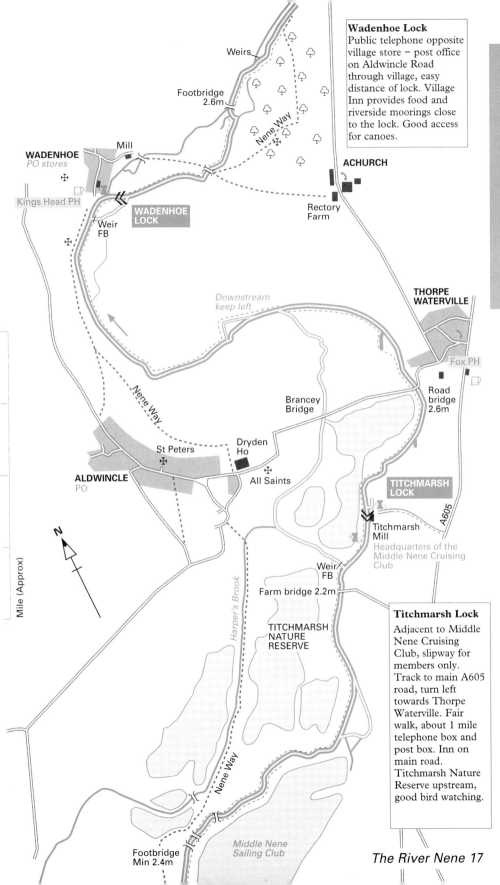

Weirs

Footbridge
2.6m

Nene Way

**Wadenhoe Lock**
Public telephone opposite
village store – post office
on Aldwincle Road
through village, easy
distance of lock. Village
Inn provides food and
riverside moorings close
to the lock. Good access
for canoes.

**WADENHOE**
*PO stores*

Mill

**ACHURCH**

Rectory
Farm

*Kings Head PH*

**WADENHOE
LOCK**

Weir
FB

**THORPE
WATERVILLE**

*Fox PH*

*Downstream
keep left*

Road
bridge
2.6m

Nene Way

Brancey
Bridge

A605

Dryden
Ho

St Peters

**ALDWINCLE**
*PO*

All Saints

**TITCHMARSH
LOCK**

Titchmarsh
Mill
*Headquarters of the
Middle Nene Cruising
Club*

1

Mile (Approx)

N

Harper's Brook

Weir
FB

Farm bridge 2.2m

**TITCHMARSH
NATURE
RESERVE**

0

Nene Way

**Titchmarsh Lock**
Adjacent to Middle
Nene Cruising
Club, slipway for
members only.
Track to main A605
road, turn left
towards Thorpe
Waterville. Fair
walk, about 1 mile
telephone box and
post box. Inn on
main road.
Titchmarsh Nature
Reserve upstream,
good bird watching.

*Middle Nene
Sailing Club*

Footbridge
Min 2.4m

*The River Nene 17*

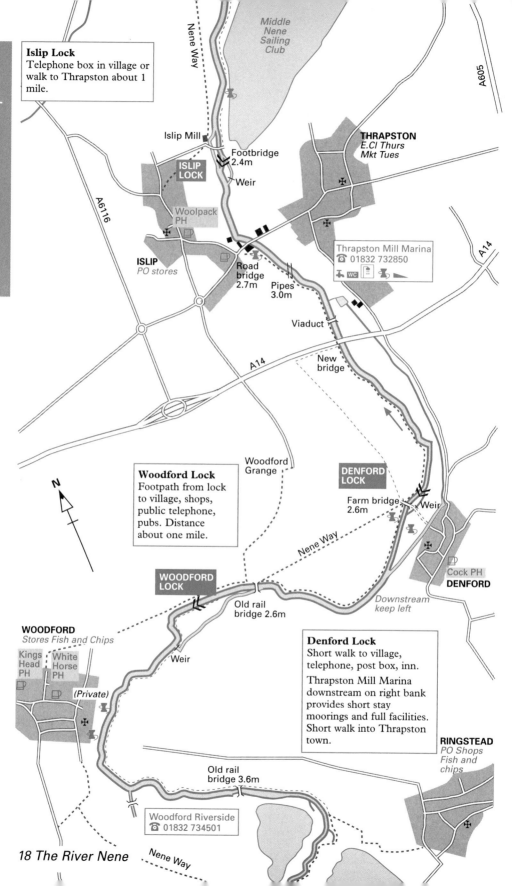

**Islip Lock**
Telephone box in village or walk to Thrapston about 1 mile.

Middle Nene Sailing Club

Nene Way

A605

Islip Mill

Footbridge 2.4m

Weir

**THRAPSTON**
E.Cl Thurs
Mkt Tues

**ISLIP LOCK**

Woolpack PH

A6116

**ISLIP**
*PO stores*

Road bridge 2.7m

Pipes 3.0m

Thrapston Mill Marina
☎ 01832 732850

A14

Viaduct

A14

New bridge

**Woodford Lock**
Footpath from lock to village, shops, public telephone, pubs. Distance about one mile.

Woodford Grange

**DENFORD LOCK**

Farm bridge 2.6m

Weir

Nene Way

N

**WOODFORD LOCK**

Old rail bridge 2.6m

Cock PH
**DENFORD**

*Downstream keep left*

**WOODFORD**
*Stores Fish and Chips*

Kings Head PH

White Horse PH

(Private)

Weir

**Denford Lock**
Short walk to village, telephone, post box, inn.

Thrapston Mill Marina downstream on right bank provides short stay moorings and full facilities. Short walk into Thrapston town.

**RINGSTEAD**
*PO Shops Fish and chips*

Old rail bridge 3.6m

Woodford Riverside
☎ 01832 734501

*18 The River Nene*

Nene Way

Nene Way

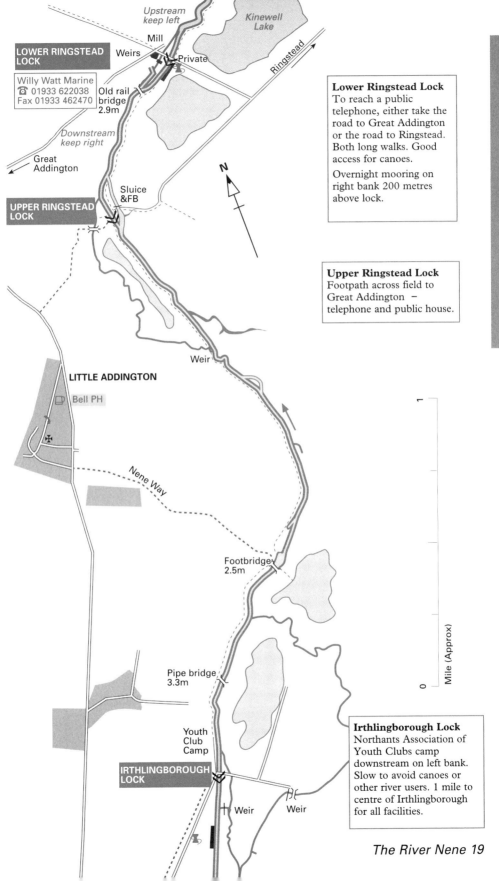

**Upstream keep left**

Kinewell Lake

Mill

Weirs

Ringstead

**LOWER RINGSTEAD LOCK**

Private

Willy Watt Marine
☎ 01933 622038
Fax 01933 462470

Old rail bridge 2.9m

*Downstream keep right*

Great Addington

Sluice &FB

N

**UPPER RINGSTEAD LOCK**

**Lower Ringstead Lock**
To reach a public telephone, either take the road to Great Addington or the road to Ringstead. Both long walks. Good access for canoes.

Overnight mooring on right bank 200 metres above lock.

**Upper Ringstead Lock**
Footpath across field to Great Addington – telephone and public house.

Weir

**LITTLE ADDINGTON**

Bell PH

Nene Way

Footbridge 2.5m

1

Mile (Approx)

0

Pipe bridge 3.3m

Youth Club Camp

**IRTHLINGBOROUGH LOCK**

Weir    Weir

**Irthlingborough Lock**
Northants Association of Youth Clubs camp downstream on left bank. Slow to avoid canoes or other river users. 1 mile to centre of Irthlingborough for all facilities.

*The River Nene 19*

Rushden&
Diamonds
Football
Club

Weir
Road bridge 2.9m
Use largest arch

**IRTHLINGBOROUGH**
*PO Shops*

Doc Marten's
Factory
Shop

High
road
bridge

**HIGHAM
FERRERS**

A6

**HIGHAM
LOCK**

Nene Way

Farm bridge
2.1m

A45

B571

*Gravel
Pits*

*Gravel
Pit*

**Higham Lock**
Nature reserve on both banks
with good bird watching. Walk
to Higham Ferrers for shops,
pubs etc. Good canoe access
from Wharfe Road.

Footbridge

Sewage
Works

Conveyor
bridge
3.6m

Weir

RUSHDEN

**DITCHFORD
LOCK**

*Skew
Bridge
Ski Lake*

Club
House

Ditchford bridge
2.8m

*Ditchford
Lake*

A45

N

Weir

*Downstream
keep right*

**Ditchford Lock**
Radial gate and
pointing doors. No
telephone within
easy walking
distance.
Emergencies – AW
Broadholme Sewage
Treatment Works on
the left bank.

20

High rail
bridge

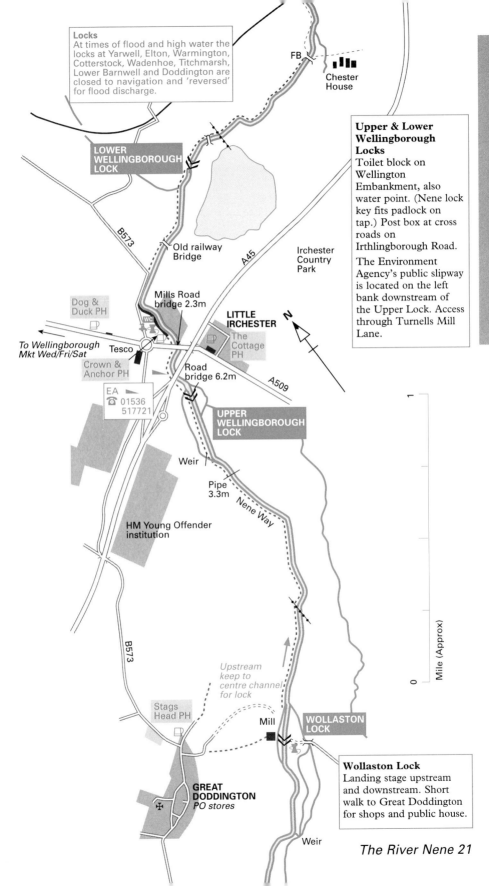

**Locks**
At times of flood and high water the locks at Yarwell, Elton, Warmington, Cotterstock, Wadenhoe, Titchmarsh, Lower Barnwell and Doddington are closed to navigation and 'reversed' for flood discharge.

FB

Chester House

LOWER WELLINGBOROUGH LOCK

**Upper & Lower Wellingborough Locks**
Toilet block on Wellington Embankment, also water point. (Nene lock key fits padlock on tap.) Post box at cross roads on Irthlingborough Road.

The Environment Agency's public slipway is located on the left bank downstream of the Upper Lock. Access through Turnells Mill Lane.

B573

Old railway Bridge

A45

Irchester Country Park

Mills Road bridge 2.3m

LITTLE IRCHESTER

The Cottage PH

N

Dog & Duck PH

WC

To Wellingborough
Mkt Wed/Fri/Sat

Tesco

Crown & Anchor PH

Road bridge 6.2m

A509

EA ☎ 01536 517721

UPPER WELLINGBOROUGH LOCK

Weir

Pipe 3.3m

Nene Way

HM Young Offender institution

B573

Upstream keep to centre channel for lock

Stags Head PH

Mill

WOLLASTON LOCK

**Wollaston Lock**
Landing stage upstream and downstream. Short walk to Great Doddington for shops and public house.

GREAT DODDINGTON
PO stores

Weir

Mile (Approx)

1

0

*The River Nene 21*

**GREAT DODDINGTON** *PO stores*

Summerleys Nature Reserve

Nene Way

Footbridge 2.3m

N

*Upstream keep right*

Road bridge 2.4m

Sluices

**DODDINGTON LOCK**

Hardwater Mill

*Downstream keep left*

Weir

A45

*Upstream keep left*

Gravel pits

Nene Way

Mill

**EARLS BARTON LOCK**

Weir

Gantry 3.3m

**EARLS BARTON** *PO stores PH's*

**WHITE MILLS LOCK**

Dunkleys Restaurant & PH

Weir

*Downstream keep left*

Weir

Farm Bridge 2.6m

Nene Way

**Locks**
At times of flood and high water the locks at Yarwell, Elton, Warmington, Cotterstock, Wadenhoe, Titchmarsh, Lower Barnwell and Doddington are closed to navigation and 'reversed' for flood discharge.

**WHISTON LOCK**

To Whiston

Weir

**Doddington Lock**
Half mile to main road, turn right at cross roads to Great Doddington village or use nene Way. Post office, shops, call box.

**Earls Barton Lock**
Centre of Earls Barton, 1½ miles but no easy access.

**White Mills Lock**
Emergencies only telephone at nearby Garden Centre. All facilities at Earls Barton. Walk of 1¼ miles.

**Whiston Lock**
Nearest telephone is in Whiston village – long walk. Post box in wall by bus stop. No shops.

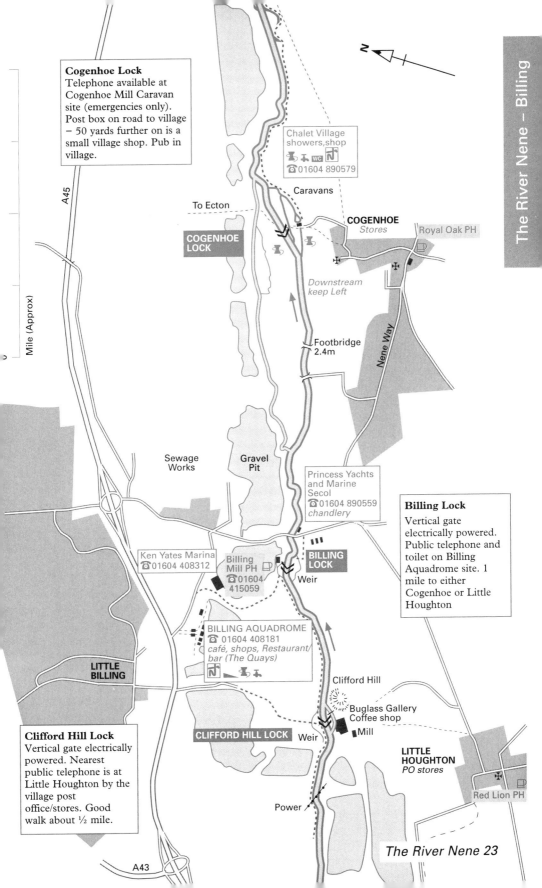

N

**Cogenhoe Lock**
Telephone available at
Cogenhoe Mill Caravan
site (emergencies only).
Post box on road to village
– 50 yards further on is a
small village shop. Pub in
village.

A45

Mile (Approx)

Chalet Village
showers, shop
☎ 01604 890579

Caravans

To Ecton

**COGENHOE
LOCK**

**COGENHOE**
*Stores*

Royal Oak PH

*Downstream
keep Left*

Footbridge
2.4m

Nene Way

Sewage
Works

Gravel
Pit

Princess Yachts
and Marine
Secol
☎ 01604 890559
*chandlery*

**Billing Lock**

Vertical gate
electrically powered.
Public telephone and
toilet on Billing
Aquadrome site. 1
mile to either
Cogenhoe or Little
Houghton

Ken Yates Marina
☎ 01604 408312

Billing
Mill PH
☎ 01604
415059

**BILLING
LOCK**

Weir

**LITTLE
BILLING**

BILLING AQUADROME
☎ 01604 408181
*café, shops, Restaurant/
bar (The Quays)*

Clifford Hill

Buglass Gallery
Coffee shop

**CLIFFORD HILL LOCK**

Weir

Mill

**LITTLE
HOUGHTON**
*PO stores*

**Clifford Hill Lock**
Vertical gate electrically
powered. Nearest
public telephone is at
Little Houghton by the
village post
office/stores. Good
walk about ½ mile.

Power

Red Lion PH

*The River Nene 23*

A43

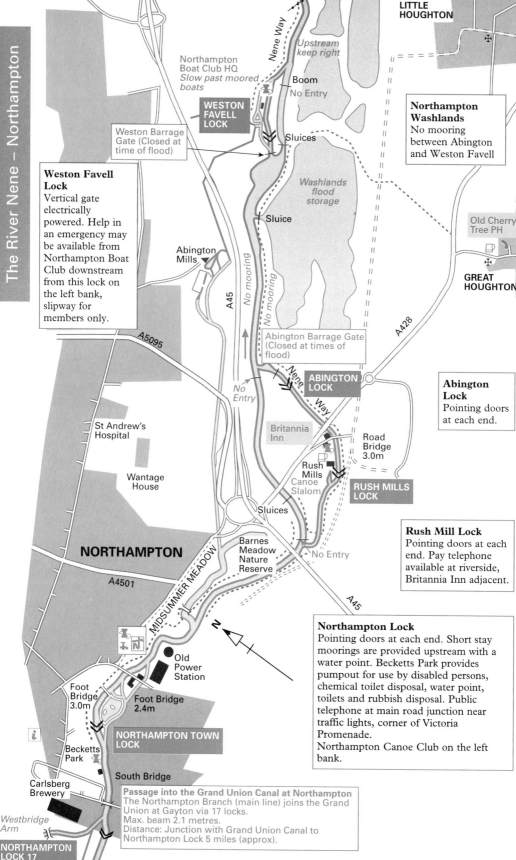

**LITTLE HOUGHTON**

Nene Way

*Upstream keep right*

Northampton Boat Club HQ
*Slow past moored boats*

Boom
No Entry

**WESTON FAVELL LOCK**

Weston Barrage Gate (Closed at time of flood)

Sluices

**Northampton Washlands**
No mooring between Abington and Weston Favell

Sluice

*Washlands flood storage*

Old Cherry Tree PH

**GREAT HOUGHTON**

**Weston Favell Lock**
Vertical gate electrically powered. Help in an emergency may be available from Northampton Boat Club downstream from this lock on the left bank, slipway for members only.

Abington Mills

A45

*No mooring*

A5095

Abington Barrage Gate (Closed at times of flood)

A428

*No Entry*

Nene Way

**ABINGTON LOCK**

St Andrew's Hospital

Britannia Inn

Road Bridge 3.0m

**Abington Lock**
Pointing doors at each end.

Wantage House

Rush Mills
Canoe Slalom

**RUSH MILLS LOCK**

Sluices

**NORTHAMPTON**

A4501

Barnes Meadow Nature Reserve

No Entry

A45

**Rush Mill Lock**
Pointing doors at each end. Pay telephone available at riverside, Britannia Inn adjacent.

MIDSUMMER MEADOW

N

**Northampton Lock**
Pointing doors at each end. Short stay moorings are provided upstream with a water point. Becketts Park provides pumpout for use by disabled persons, chemical toilet disposal, water point, toilets and rubbish disposal. Public telephone at main road junction near traffic lights, corner of Victoria Promenade.
Northampton Canoe Club on the left bank.

Old Power Station

Foot Bridge 3.0m

Foot Bridge 2.4m

**NORTHAMPTON TOWN LOCK**

Becketts Park

South Bridge

Carlsberg Brewery

*Westbridge Arm*

**NORTHAMPTON LOCK 17**

**Passage into the Grand Union Canal at Northampton**
The Northampton Branch (main line) joins the Grand Union at Gayton via 17 locks.
Max. beam 2.1 metres.
Distance: Junction with Grand Union Canal to Northampton Lock 5 miles (approx).

**NORTHAMPTON**

Foot Bridge 2.4m

MIDSUMMER MEADOW

River Nene

Old Power Station

Foot Bridge 3.0m

Sluices

A508

Becketts Park

**NORTHAMPTON TOWN LOCK**

**Northampton, No.17 Cotton End Lock**
Joining the Nene from the Grand Union Canal, passing under Northampton South Bridge.

Carlsberg Brewery

South Bridge

A5123

**NORTHAMPTON LOCK 17**

Cotton End

Stn

Westbridge Arm

A43

A428

**Passage into the Grand Union Canal at Northampton**
The Northampton Branch (main line) joins the Grand Union at Gayton via 17 locks.
Max. beam 2.1 metres.
Distance: Junction with Grand Union Canal to Northampton Lock 5 miles (approx).

Railway

Grand Union Canal (Northampton Arm)

Nene Way

**HUNSBY LOCK 16**

R. Nene

Railway

A45

Hunsbury Hall Country Park

N

Northampton Town FC

Duston Mill

**HARDINGSTONE LOCK 15**

A45

1

Mile (Approx)

St Crispins Hospital (Tower)

River Nene

A43

**WOOTTON LOCK 14**

0

M1

To Towcester

Services

**ROTHERSTHORPE LOCKS 1 - 13**

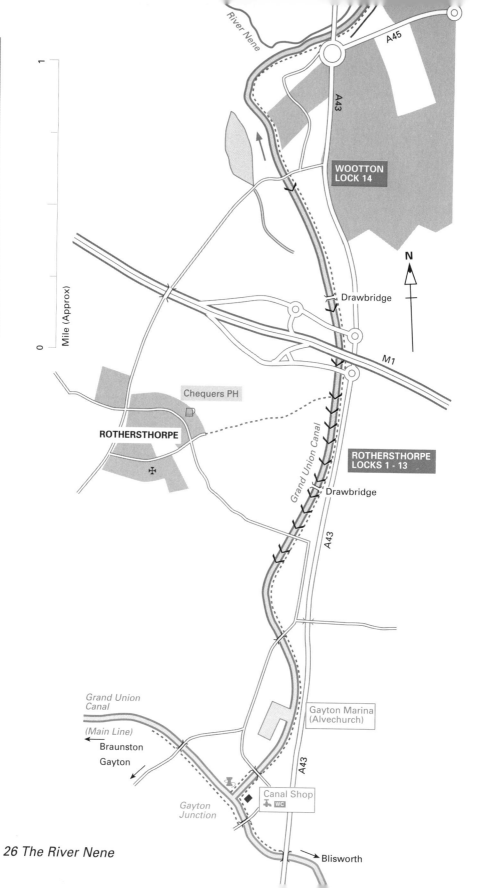

1

0

Mile (Approx)

River Nene

A45

A43

WOOTTON LOCK 14

N

Drawbridge

M1

Chequers PH

ROTHERSTHORPE

Grand Union Canal

ROTHERSTHORPE LOCKS 1 - 13

Drawbridge

A43

Grand Union Canal

(Main Line)

Braunston

Gayton

Gayton Marina (Alvechurch)

A43

Gayton Junction

Canal Shop
WC

Blisworth

*26 The River Nene*